Girls' World
All My Pets

Phidal

CHARLIE

Come join the Girls' World and read about all kinds of fun activities!
This sticker book is for girls only! You can place
the reusable stickers anywhere you like.
After completing all the games, use the last
page to create a story of your own.

5 years and up.

Produced and Published by Phidal Publishing Inc.
5740 Ferrier, Montreal, Quebec, Canada H4P 1M7
All rights reserved.
Printed in Italy.
www.phidal.com

ISBN: 2-7643-0142-1

*We acknowledge the financial support of the government of Canada
through the BPIDP for our publishing activities.*

Pets in Place

Help these animals find their friends by grouping them with your stickers.

Bathtime!

This naughty dog was rolling in the mud! Time for a bath!
Help Jackie find all the things she needs to clean her muddy puppy.

Playtime

Animals like to play different games, but some of them have forgotten where they put their toys. Can you match up the pets with their missing playthings?

Sunny Days!

It's a beautiful day in the park! Everyone will bring their pets outside to play.
Use your stickers to decorate the scene.

Time for Treats

Animals have favorite foods just like you. These animals are hungry!
Will you feed them what they like to eat best?

Perfect Pairs

Have you ever noticed that pets and their owners sometimes look alike?
Use your stickers and see if you can tell who goes together.

Time For Bed

It's been an exciting day playing with so many animals! Now all your friends with fins, feathers, and fur are sleepy. Can you tuck them into their own beds and say goodnight?

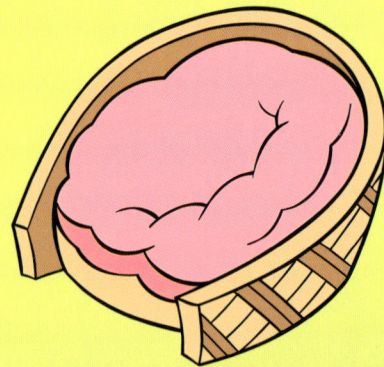

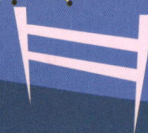